NOT A *MARKETING* BOOK!

Marketing ideas for this age

Siddharth Deshmukh

Visuals by Moina Abdul

INDIA · SINGAPORE · MALAYSIA

ISBN 979-8-89632-406-5

Not A Marketing Book

If marketers thought differently, marketing can become better.
This is NOT a regular book on marketing.
Reading these notes and using them intelligently will make you a
better marketer. Whether you are a novice or an experienced hand
at marketing. And even if you just want to use *better* marketing
thinking for your success.

These notes will make you think differently about the familiar, like:
Customers that a*dvertise* (yes!)
Advertisers that Platforms *reject* (biting the hand that feeds them)
Platforms that *choose* Brands(It's all about the feeling)
Brands that are created by Sales Activities (brand building done
differently)... and more

These collected insights are from observations, conversations and
learnings. Distilled across markets, practitioners, academics,
students, teachers... and sceptics about the discipline of marketing.

I'd recommend that you read a note or three
When you have a minute or two
For a flash of inspiration.
(Or, just read it over a Saturday afternoon. Both work.)

Don't choose your platform, let your platform choose you

You want to build your personal brand- and are wondering which platform to choose. Don't. Instead, do this.

Get on all platforms.
Get on everything. X, LinkedIn, the Rotary club (I mean all platforms!)
Keep an open mind.
Ask: "How do I *feel* on this platform?"

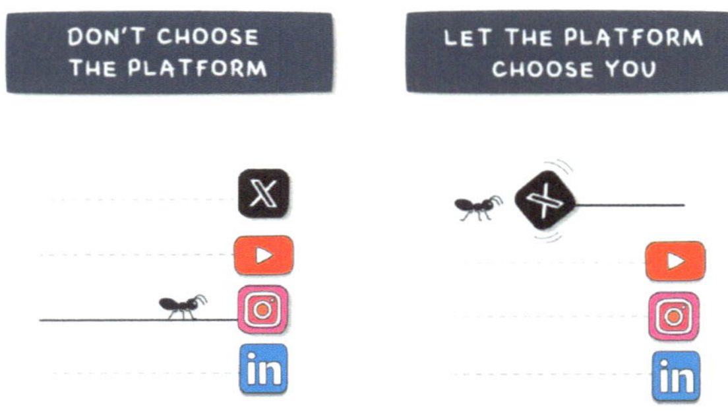

You may think that the answer lies in a logical combination of things:
- The people on the platform are like you
- You know that your customers/clients are present and they are in a listening frame of mind,
- You find the features easy to use,
- What's created and shared on the platform is something you like and can consistently participate in...

But how you *feel* is not logical.
Feel that you belong? Feel welcome?
Do you experience a sense of flow?
Yes?

Welcome, your platform has just chosen you.

Market yourself before you launch anything else

A lot of marketers feel that the product, the service, the business model, and the business itself must be **near readiness** for even thinking about a soft launch.

They are wasting time.
Don't be like them.
Don't waste time NOT marketing yourself while you wait for your product and business to be ready.

You need to find an audience that:
… *understands* and appreciates what you do.
…vibes with the *values* you stand for.
…*loves* what your unique voice has to say.
…respects the "*purpose and meaning*" hill you'd be willing to die on.
…will *support* whatever you launch.

When you're connected like this with your audience AND then you launch your stuff, the impact will be far BIGGER.
This takes time, effort, and many, many pivots.
You need a "product- market" fit, first, for **yourself**.
Use the time you've got and get it.

People don't want to think about your toothpaste. We want Vacation- Ready Teeth.

We don't want to think of mundane things.

We want to think about our day, our coming weekend, our impending job interview, when we brush our teeth.

We don't want to think about your toothpaste, Mr. Marketer. Anything else is better.

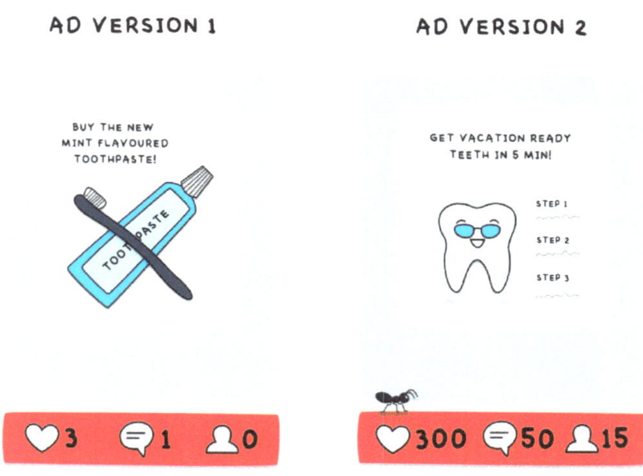

Sure, we may get a bit excited about a new flavour/whitening ingredient/cavity fighter when we're buying groceries.

If you're lucky.

(Continued)

Sure, we may get a bit excited about a new flavour/whitening ingredient/cavity fighter when we're buying groceries.

If you're lucky.

But mostly, we don't want to think about your toothpaste.
We want to quickly turn into a habit anything that can be turned into a habit. We don't want that cognitive overload.

So why in the world does your brand of toothpaste have a social media page? Nobody cares except your agency and you.

Make content around "vacation-ready teeth", and maybe we'll think about your toothpaste.

Investing in getting attention is better than day trading in it

If you believe "Any publicity is good publicity",
You'll try to capture and retain attention on *undervalued* platforms,
therefore getting more bang for your buck.

This means:

Focus on *using trends* (what content will gain attention)
Align with the popular and under-priced platforms and influencers (be where it is all inexpensively happening)

If ATTENTION was a stock in the exchange, you are DAY TRADING in it.

These are good tactics. No one denies that. But it ain't enough.

Can we go *beyond* the algorithms of the day?
Can we create a strong, consistent *signal* about the value of your brand?
On platforms that your customers will actually *listen* to you?

This means a few things:
-Perhaps going for the more expensive platform
-The quality of the message is paramount,
-Posting fewer times, with the right kind of messengers.

You will be consistently INVESTING in attracting a certain kind of ATTENTION from a certain kind of customer.

Yes, Investing in attention doesn't have the same excitement as day trading in it.

But ask Warren Buffet about investing money, and he'll tell you- **the more boring it seems, the more effective it is- in the long term.**

Perhaps, be less like Gary V, and more like Warren Buffet.

The customer is always on a journey

The customer is never *still*. She is always moving.
She's either busy in the physical world, or in her *mind*.
She is choosing, evaluating, switching off, switching on and splitting her attention across various aspects of her life.

She's not just aware of what you're offering.
She's considering your *competition*.
She's interested in alternatives.
She's flitting back and forth between *choices*.

She's not like this once in a while. **She's like this all the time**.
There's a storm of thoughts, ideas, emotions and action surrounding her. A good marketer can see that she is never a *blank* canvas available exclusively for your brand to speak with.

If you create communication that talks to her as if she is static and/or receptive to your brand. You've lost. The customer is always on a journey. Hop on the train she's on, adjust to the pace, grin through the bumps and look at what she sees.
Your communication better be different on YouTube, on TV, on OOH, on FM, on…

Change up and match up. *Your brand then has half a chance.*

The customer is both stupid and intelligent.

ACT 1
"Why are you chewing gum before a meal… won't you lose your appetite?"
"*Oh- I just wanted to pass time..*"

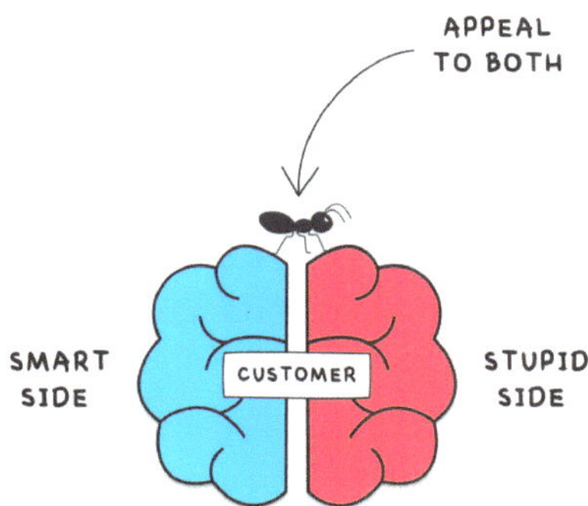

ACT 2
"Why are you chewing gum before a meal… won't you lose your appetite?"
"Oh- I just wanted to supress my appetite, *I'm on a diet..*"

Tell me you haven't been very stupid at times:

Making irrational decisions that you regret later
Missing the obvious thing
Aggravating people around you on a bad day

We've all been like that.
We all will be like that in the future.

(Continued)

Tell me you haven't been very intelligent at times:

Surprising yourself and people around you with your amazing solutions
Using smart hacks and being in flow
Connecting with people effectively

We've all been like that.
We all will be like that in the future.

Is it *Stupid Sid* or *Smart Sid* making those buying decisions?
(Of course, Stupid Sid will rationalise decisions post purchase to make himself appear like Smart Sid)

 A marketer should understand which part of the human being is showing up.

The next time you sell Insurance, Chewing gum, or anything, really- try out communication options that talk to the silly and sensible sides.

Test both out -in different contexts.

Let's celebrate the chance to connect with customers in more than one way.

Customer Segments exist only in a marketer's mind

In a marketer's *mind*, customers belong to neat segments.

A segment is full of:
-Customers or prospects of a certain age,
-living in a certain place,
-doing certain jobs,
-having a predictable family,
-who do specific things on weekends with a set of fixed attitudes.

This makes targeting these customers logical, smart and effective –
On *paper*.

However, the real world is chaotic. People have:
- messy lives,
-complicated relationships,
-weird work gigs.
-and sometimes, have no idea what they'll do on a weekend.

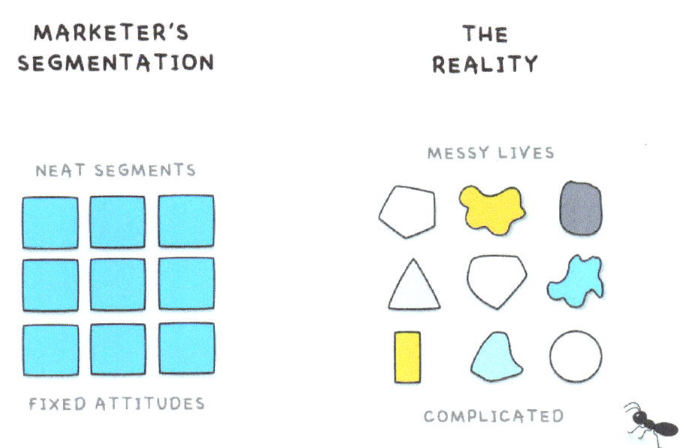

(Continued)

Following segmentation strictly can lead to marketers communicating to customers who don't *exist*.

Why do marketers segment, then?

Marketers face uncertainty at their job. That's why they want order instead of chaos. They want to justify things at work. Make things as scientific as possible. And of course, you can't target the whole population.

Here's what I recommend:
Use segmentation as a starting point.
And then, why not look for differences in the segment you have chosen?
You can then personalise as much as possible to individual customers.

It wasn't possible when the concept of segmentation was first created. But with AI and tech, there's no excuse for predictable, boring, marketing communication that doesn't work.

Start with segmentation, but get out of it pronto, Dear Marketer.

The best way to be a marketer is to not be one

Marketers need to be *pretenders*.
Pretending to be accountants, chefs, insurance salesmen, astronauts, scientists, and every profession that matters to their work.

They need to have fun.

They need to know:
-what it is to be drunk,
-to be sober,
-to goof off,
-to be serious,
-to watch, listen, read,
have a hobby,
-be a leftist, be a right winger,
be open …

Think about it.

If you think, feel, and "be" a marketer, you will always be in your **own** skin.

There is nothing more *alienating* to a customer than the kind of work this kind of marketer will offer.

You will find it too hard to analyse data, to craft compelling messages, to be convincing, to get a sale.

The best way to be a marketer is to get out of the skin of a marketer's profession.

Calling marketing "digital" is akin to calling a bulb electric

The humble bulb that you need to sometimes change on your bedside table lamp has an interesting history.

In 1879, it was called the *"electric light utility"* because it was in competition with gas light utilities.

It slowly morphed into an electric bulb, and in 2024, when you go to a shop that sells them, you're probably asked whether you want long lasting LED bulbs, or a choice between yellow/white.

I'm sure 25 years later, it will be called something else.

What's this got to do with *Digital Marketing*?

Plenty.

(Continued)

Digital Marketing, when it started a fe decades back, *differentiated* itself from "traditional, conventional" marketing that used mainstream media.

It provided excitement because of efficiencies, new data driven learnings, and new types of customer interactions(social, search, e-commerce, and more)

Today, *all* marketing is either completely digitally driven, or has a significant digital component, or is always talking to a customer deep into the digital world.

Why do we still insist on calling it Digital Marketing?

We're living in the past. Competing with ghosts. Using a differentiation which doesn't work.

All marketing is digital. It is also commoditised to such an extent that it has become the category.

Today, the differentiation is "*AI driven marketing*". Tomorrow, it will be something else.

The *marketing* of Marketing by marketers is an interesting case study.

Use AI to be as human as possible

If you see the *increase* in content of late, especially on social networks like LinkedIn, you see the ineffectiveness of AI driven marketing.

You can recognise it a mile away. I'm betting that 8 times out of 10, you can recognise AI driven content.

Why can we recognise it? We can, because as customers, we have inbuilt b*******t detectors.

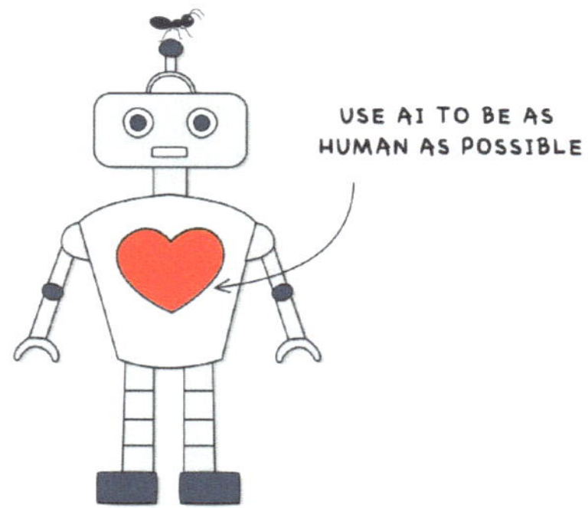

Good content, written, edited, or tweaked by a human being, connects in a very different way.You can recognise the impact and effort behind it by how you FEEL about it. For example, you already know, by now, that this book uses no AI.

Most marketers are using AI to create MORE content, rather than BETTER content. They are using AI in a sloppy, lazy, uninspired manner. I'd suggest a different approach.

Let's do the hard work instead of saying "create me a LinkedIn post on this topic/ trend". Let's use AI to give us better customer *insights*.
Help us know our customer's *language*.
Allow us to increase empathy, trust, and *humanity*.

Use AI **not** to make us super human, but as human as possible.

Bake your marketing in the product

Let's imagine that you are baking a cake for someone you love. For their birthday.

You carefully mix all the ingredients, use their favourite recipe, and ensure it comes out just right, and use attractive frosting for a beautiful, personalised message on top. You even shoot a time-lapsed video of you doing this and will post it later on your Instagram.

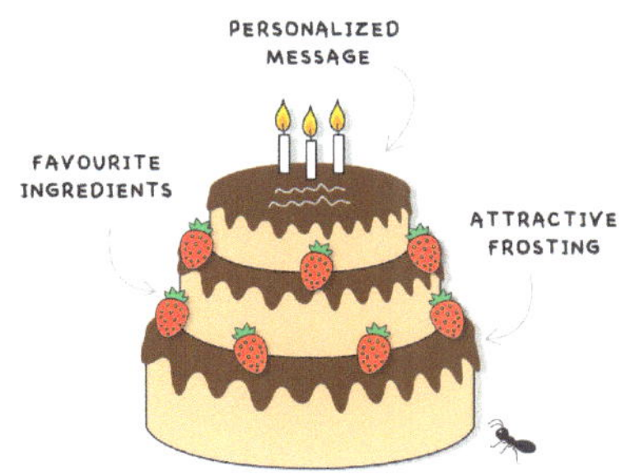

You've literally *baked your marketing* in the product.
There's a multi- layered, positive emotion generating story right there for the one you love (and for everyone else who's involved!)
So now tell me:

Why wouldn't you do this with your meditation app?
Perhaps add some ASMR to the experience that encourages more stickiness. Or encourage group meditations(Satsangs)

Your new pop up food stall?
Add a candlelit table going at a premium, for a budding romance.
Or waft some amazingly appetizing food smells outside.

Marketing isn't an **afterthought** once the product is "finished".
Every *memorable* product needs to have marketing baked *into* the product features.

You may need to market a product for its service and market a service as a product

This is indeed a *strange* thing, and only an example or two can prove it.

Let's take a product:

Perhaps a SaaS, or even an electronic gadget.
How does this kind of product often market itself?
It focuses on, perhaps, after sales handholding, or 24 hour tech support.
The product *highlights* its service elements to differentiate.

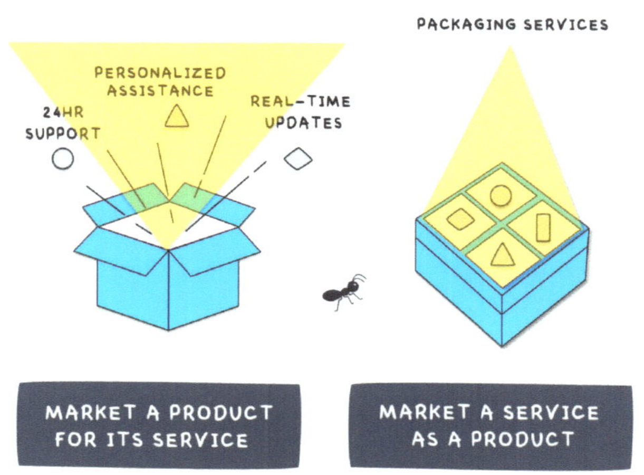

(Continued)

Let's take a service:

Perhaps an agency or consulting firm.
How does this service often market itself?
It creates some sort of product around its service- perhaps a proprietary model, or a licensed framework.
The service "*productises*" some of its elements and highlights them to differentiate.

Why does this happen, though?

Perhaps the answer is that the customer doesn't give a rat's a** about whether you have a product or a service.
She wants something that solves her need entirely, and the best one out of the lot.

In a world where you have to stand out and avoid being commoditised:
You might need to market your product for its service, and market your service as a *product*.

Marketing exists to kill sales

What we learn in B-school and tomes written on marketing:

Marketing helps sales by generating and nurturing demand. Marketing teams and sales teams are integral to each other- they complement each other, make each other *complete*.

What we un-learn in reality:
Most marketing teams in an organisation are in *constant battle* with the sales teams.

I wondered why the deep animosity exists.

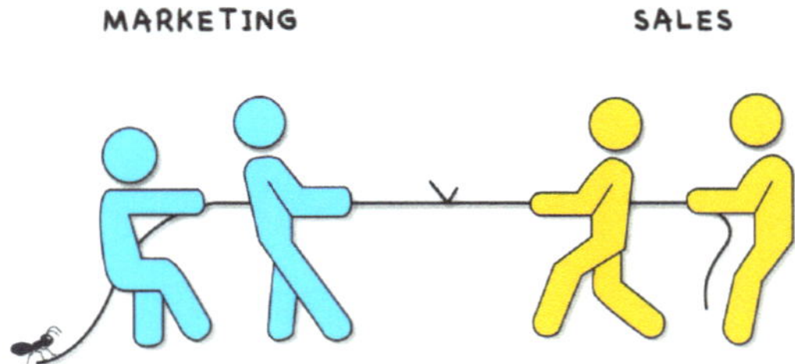

(Continued)

I had concluded that this is because a lot of sales teams consider marketing "woo-woo"; focusing on *abstract strategic* things(long term brand building).

Maybe the more *tactically oriented* sales teams want something else (promotions, discounts, offers) which marketing teams don't give.

Sure. Maybe. There's something there, of course.
But now I suspect that the reason is deeper than this.

Perhaps, the ultimate role of marketing is to *generate* so much demand with all of its work that the importance and need of a salesperson is reduced and ultimately *redundant*.

More precisely- the marketing function in any organisation eventually exists to **kill** the sales function.

Of course, this reality is never fully realised, but the two functions and teams do recognise this *somewhere deep* within themselves.

The battlelines are always drawn.

At best, Marketing and Sales are frenemies.
They will *uneasily* co-exist and smile at each other, but sneer when the other walks away.

Most great marketers are never found working in marketing

Don't we often say " Oh, she's such a great marketer" or " He really knows how to persuade"….

And *9 times out of 10*, we are talking of people who aren't in the so called "marketing" department.

Often, they are politicians.
Sometimes, film stars.
Or Start-up founders.
CEO's. Youtubers. Even some chefs.

There's a percentage of these who are *natural born* marketers. They innately know the craft of persuasion and the art of seduction.

(Continued)

There's also quite a few who have *transitioned* beyond "Marketing" careers.
They've added new skills and capabilities, and have advanced to general management/some other function which they find *more* rewarding or compelling. (CEO's, Sales Heads, Business Consultants, Professors, to name a few)

A lot of them have taken this route because of a reason.
Their experience in a marketing career has left them *unfulfilled*.
They've found out that they are not central to their workplace- because the marketing department is seen as a *supporting* or staff function.

They rebel against being undervalued and considered kind of lightweight.

But trust me, they are marketers alright.

They bring all of their marketing skills to their new game as well, whatever it may be. And they are noticed by the rest of the world.

Is your ambition to be known as a great marketer?
Perhaps your ambition will *lead you out* of marketing as well.

Advertising tries to be authentic while customers fake it on social media

The system has *flipped*.
We live in strange times.

The speed at which this has happened is unbelievable. It has happened so *seamlessly*, we've not only accepted it but embraced it.

Customers:
Once, the world courted them through ads.
Now they are the advertisers, courting the world to look at them.
All of us signal "larger than life distinctiveness" to *stand out*.

(Continued)

Advertisers:
Once, ads were courting customers through aspiration.
Now, ads are desperately trying to be real.
 All advertising says "we are just as real as you, connected and concerned with everything that bother you" to *blend in*.

Why has the system flipped?
Social media, of course. We know that.

What should the smart marketer do about this?

Incentivise customers to advertise for you, they'll do a better job of it than an ad trying to be authentic.
But be scrupulous.

Spend your traditional advertising budget into supporting a popular movement or cause that signals your authenticity to people.
You'll feel a *new support* for your brand.

If all your customers wear your ripped pair of jeans, you are serving conformists who think they are rebels

There's that one rebel who wore that ripped pair of jeans first. She had different makeup, and her earrings were cool and mysterious, too. She was into exploring her taste in clothes and accessorizing in a new way. Visiting thrift shops before they became cool.

That was your *innovator* in action, vibing with your product.

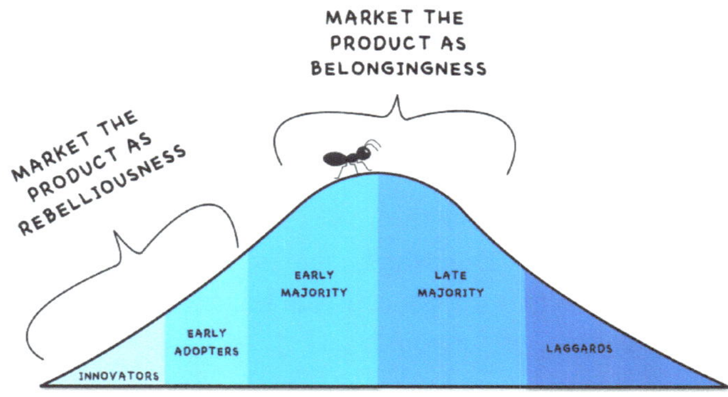

Then came the ones who just connected with her and the emotion it represented. They loved the rebelliousness and the feeling of enthusiastic participation.

(Continued)

They were your *early adopters*, joining the innovator early in the curve.

By the time the *early majority* started wearing ripped jeans, you knew that everyone was into it.

There was little risk involved, and the market had reached *tipping point* to ensure that people who wore ripped jeans now were conformists rather than rebels.

The Law of Diffusion of Innovation is a marketer's ally.

It tells you exactly where you are in the lifecycle of your brand and brand's category.

It helps you *market the same product* as rebelliousness(to innovators and early adopters) or belongingness (to early and late majority).

Brands: Don't have a purpose, reflect customer values instead

Most brands need to stop finding a purpose(or mission, vision, cause or movement) for themselves that they speak *incessantly* about.

Unless that is something that they were doing before, for a long time, before they started advertising it.

Customers can *smell* the bull****
So why are brands on the this train?

The world is becoming *commoditised* quickly for brands.
We're able to rapidly replicate what our competition offers.
Our competition does the same to us.

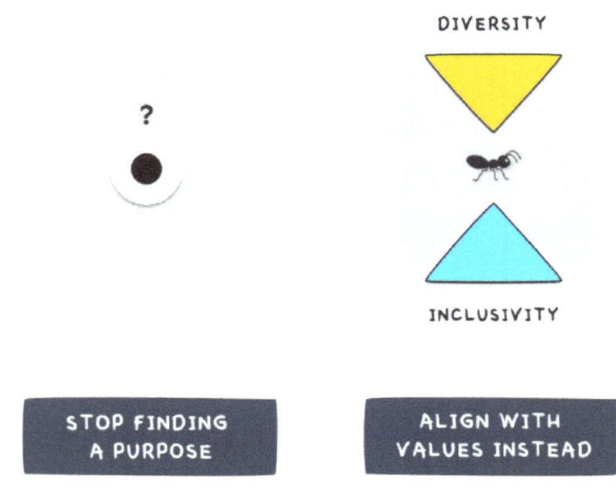

(Continued)

So Brands think that by talking of some purpose that will create an emotional connect will create a *moat* against commoditisation.

They think that their customers want to hear about this.

But will "Purpose" work for chewing gum, many software companies, and most of the products or services that come to your mind?

Nope. You know what will?

Understanding the ever changing, nuanced and complex *set of values* that your customers have.
And **aligning** your brand with them.

Nike did this really well.
It aligned with its customers by reflecting the values that they hold close to their hearts.

They supported a community(running app)
They supported inclusivity and diversity (Black Lives Matter)
They understood inspiration (Celebrity Hoardings)

They *reflected* the many values that their customers hold dear.

I'm not a Nike fan.
I'm sure they get a whole bunch of things wrong as well, but they did this one well.

No "stated" purpose.
Just Do It.

Don't convince them or confuse them to convert them

Forget the old trope: " If you can't convince them, confuse them"

Why? Because we live in an age of *information symmetry*.

It means that, through Gen AI or Search, you can potentially know what your doctor knows.
About why you aren't feeling well.
Or know as much as your professor does.
About the subject he's teaching.
Or know as much as a customer care executive does.
About the company he's representing.

(Continued)

Of course- this is "*potentially*" know, not in reality.
Experts will always know more, they have the experience.

But as paying customers, we do feel *more power* in the relationship we
have with a brand that's trying to woo us.

What does this mean for you as a marketer?

It means that the more we try to convince people the old fashioned way,
the worse of we are in…

Winning customer *trust*.

It also means the more we try and razzle-dazzle people with hyperbole
around our brand (confuse them by sexy words and pictures and
promises), the worse of we are in… guess what?

Winning customer *trust*.

Don't try and convince or confuse to *convert* the customer.

People hunger for the nuts and bolts of *truth* about your brand more
than ever.

Try being honest, direct and empathetic instead.
They'll reward you with their trust and money.

Influencers are leaders in disguise

What makes us follow certain influencers?

I'm not talking of celebrities who have a popular twitter account.
Nor am I speaking of a world renowned subject matter expert (like a chef) who builds a following on her YouTube channel.

These guys have proven skills and fame gathered *elsewhere*- not social media.

I'm talking of the **natural born storyteller**, who might be lurking in any domain- tech, beauty, lifestyle, anything.

(Continued)

They are more "come on a journey with me" rather than " I know everything about this".

They are more relatable *guide and parasocial* friend.

What makes these guys follow-worthy?

The answer, in my unresearched opinion, could be rooted in *evolution*.

Humankind succeeded because they worked in tribes.
Tribes needed leaders who could communicate well to them.

Leaders who could rally around the troops on a bad day, who could show an attainable vision, take the first brave steps in that journey.

Humankind has always gone for these kind of leaders.
Not necessarily the best at something(of course it helps!)- these people are natural born storytellers.

Even as *school going kids*, we've experienced this kind of leadership.

And we continue to experience these *leaders* on Social Media.

They're these influencers. Don't underestimate their clout.

Don't let your outcomes become your objectives

If I ask Mr. Average Joe Marketer on the street what his marketing objectives are for the year, he will answer in a quantitative, target driven manner:

"Reach "x" number of followers on the Instagram account with the new brand building campaign"
" Convert "y" of all leads into sales"
… and the like.

These are *outcomes* rather than objectives.
The tangible WHAT.

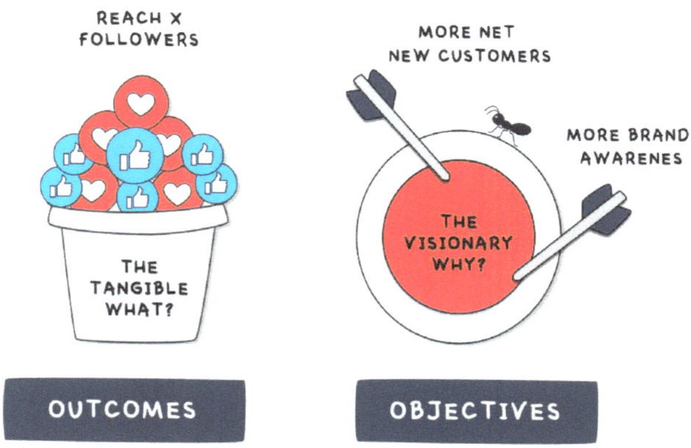

(Continued)

Objectives are, on the other hand, like:
" Make people aware and engaged with your brand in your category"
" Increase the number of net new customers"
The *Visionary* WHY.

Don't get me wrong. You need both. You need to combine objective with outcome. But don't chase your outcomes in a way that is detrimental to your objectives.

You could reach "x" number of followers on the Instagram account in a way that may not make them aware and engaged with your brand (just entertaining or shocking them for example)

Or you could reach "y" number of all leads into sales, but they may be repeat buyers instead of net new customers.

Start with Objectives. Make your Outcomes more meaningful.

All performance marketing should build brand. All brand marketing should convert customers.

A Brand is the *residue* of all perceptions about a product, service or a person at a given point of time held by your prospects and customers.

Please read that again.
THE RESIDUE of perceptions.

This residue is the sum total of perceptions at any given point in time.
Created at the top of the marketing funnel, where people are barely aware of you.
At the bottom of the funnel, where people are steps away from buying you.
And beyond- where people are actively experiencing you.

This residue comes from every *interaction* that a brand has.
Perceptions are always being made, or unmade.

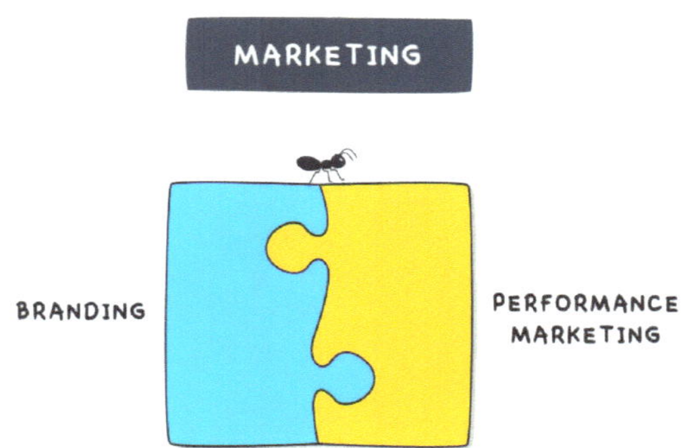

(Continued)

A strong brand is the one which is still creating the *right kind* of residue that attracts, engages and converts prospects and returning customers.

Sure, what you say to convert a person who is just about to buy you, or has already bought you is obviously going to be *different* when a person is just getting acquainted with you.

But you don't need to be *completely* different just because you are in the bottom of funnel "performance marketing" zone.

The key is to *maintain* your brand's key values even when offering deals or incentives.

If you're Apple, you shouldn't suddenly behave like Samsung. Or vice versa.

Every bit of that residue matters.

At every stage, all great marketing is always attempting to get, retain and grow customers with this residue.

It is just communicating differently based on the context.

Having 0 customers is better than having 1 customer for 3 kinds of people.

Oh, don't get me wrong.

To have one customer rather than none is a great *boost*.

It proves a lot of things:
Your offering's worth,
It confirms the price, channel of communication and distribution,
And the selection of your target segment.

And if that one customer gives you a solid testimonial, well, it's a great sign.

However, having 0 customers is great for 3 kinds of stakeholders:

A type of INVESTOR: A type of angel INVESTOR, who really likes the team , what they're doing, and what the vision and business plan is. She is buying into this, rather than the reality of 0 customers so far.

It's the *potential*.

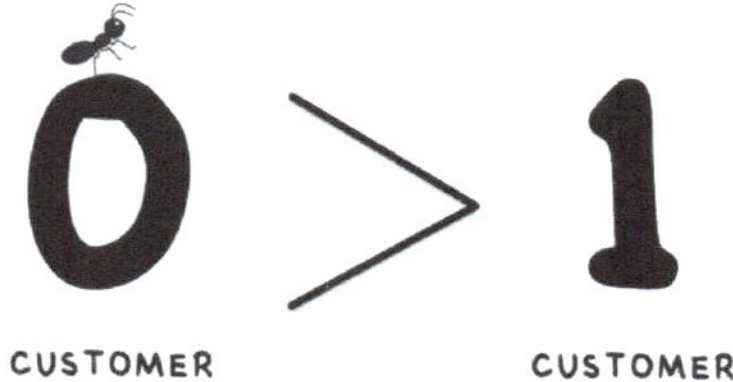

(Continued)

A type of EMPLOYEE: The early bird employee, who has joined your merry
band and wants to be part of the Rocketship before it became one.
He is sold on the journey and mission.

It's the *climb*.

A type of FOUNDER: The person with the mindset of conquering the world,
She sees things idealistically with a new set of values and solutions.

It's the dream.

These people get a dose of **reality** when they have one customer.
Then, problems arise.
How do we keep the 1 customer happy?
How do we grow this 1 to a not-so lame number?

For these guys, 0 is a better number, since it keeps them in their *La La Land.*
For everyone else, 1 is way better.

13% market share is better than 10% of it

So if you were a marketing person, and you grew your brand from- let's say 5% market share, to say 10% in a year, you'll be chuffed, right?

I mean, you have *doubled* it after all…

And then if someone comes up to you and says:
"well, that's great , but it would have been even better if it were 13%"…

You'd think that person was just nit picking.

But he'd be *right*.

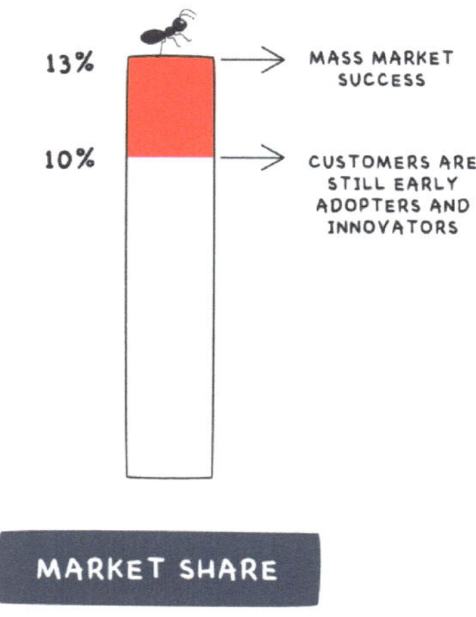

(Continued)

While doubling your market share and cornering 10% of the market is indeed noteworthy, these customers are still early adopters and innovators (based on hard core data, this, across most categories).

They just intuitively understand what you're offering, love you for what you stand for, and take a chance with you because that's who *they* are.

You haven't hit the tipping point yet.

When you hit it, you will rapidly become the market leader and shaper of your category.

More sales will rapidly follow.

Getting to 13% means wider market acceptance from the *early and late majorities.*

Early majority in a segment is *risk averse*, and when it accepts you, it does because you have been whetted long and hard enough.

Sales go through the roof.

A brand like APPLE experienced that tipping point in the early 2000's and has not looked back yet.
On the other hand, Harley Davidson's has never triumphed beyond a niche.

The 13% tipping point represents a different kind of *customer acceptance.*

Loyalty programs make customers untrustworthy

Loyalty programs make sense in *theory*.
You want to retain your existing customers and increase the money spent with you.

Laudable objectives.

But enticing them with a loyalty program where they are earning reward points of their engagement with you is a dicey proposition.

How so?

Because human beings are predictable. They understand that marketers want to lock them in.

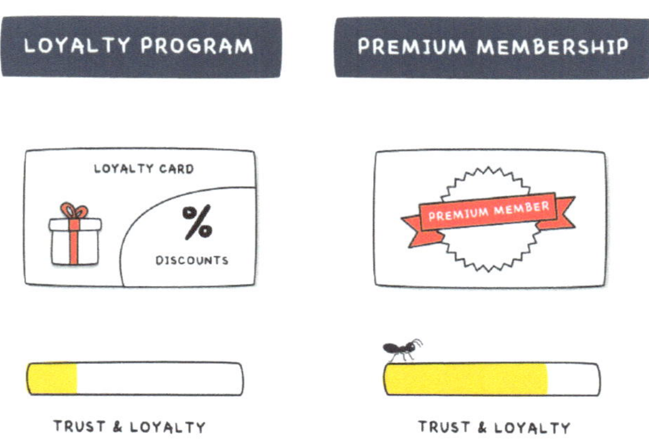

(Continued)

This makes them wonder:
Are they doing the right thing- is it wiser to be more flexible?
About carrying a bunch of cards and downloading a bunch of apps. Is it worth the hassle of time and effort?

And here's the clincher.

When they see the incentives you are offering them, they wonder how much worth they will be to your *competition*.

No wonder belonging to a loyalty program makes customers uneasy.

In fact, some intelligent companies do it the other way around. They make it a privilege for you to be their customer- and then charge a premium for it.

Think Amazon with Prime. Think One Plus with their premium community. Think Apple which doesn't do any discounting.

And then think of all the banks, telecom companies and airlines who do have *loyalty programs*.

I'd urge you to build trust with your customers without trying to *bribe* them. I'm not against Loyalty Programs, but do you really need a program for Loyalty?

Only you can answer this question for yourself.

Your brand's tone and manner is data for the subconscious.

Here's a question:

A doctor you visit is wearing *jorts*.
An accountant comes on a bike for *his meeting* with you as a client.

How do you feel?

That depends on *who you are*.

If you fall in the doctor or accountant's wheelhouse of "ideal target customers" well, you'd love them for it (even *before* they get a chance to showcase their skills)

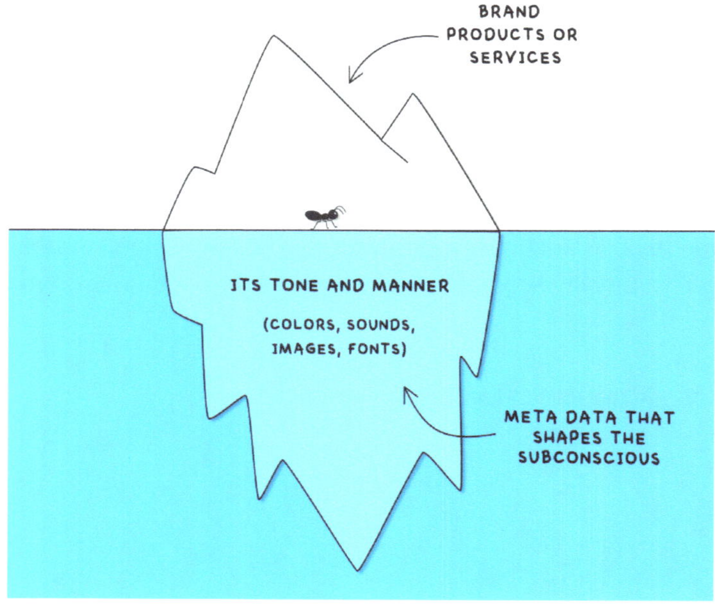

(Continued)

If you want your doctor and accountant to be sober looking and conservatively dressed, you are going to feel uneasy about them (even before they get that chance to show you how *good* they are)

All brands have a tone and manner. It is expressed through the colours, sounds, images, fonts, and everything else that isn't central to what they do.

It is how they're expressing themselves.

It does matter a lot, since the tone and manner is communicating to your subconscious, and your subconscious is making you *biased* about your choice without you knowing it.

This tone and manner is "*metadata*" (data about how data is presented) and is what the subconscious responds to.

Making sure, as a marketer, what kind of metadata is correct for your customer is not a trivial thing.

It is *more central* than what we can imagine it to be.

Don't try to measure a customer's subconscious mind, understand it instead

Marketers are always questioned about *results*- conversions, repeat purchases, or at least click through's to your website.

Whenever a brand tries to do something that doesn't connect directly with results, a lot of people consider it a *waste* of time, money and effort.

Just done to please egos and win awards.

Yes, some of it indeed is self-serving.

But a lot of this kind of indirect communication, done effectively, *shapes* a customer's subconscious mind.

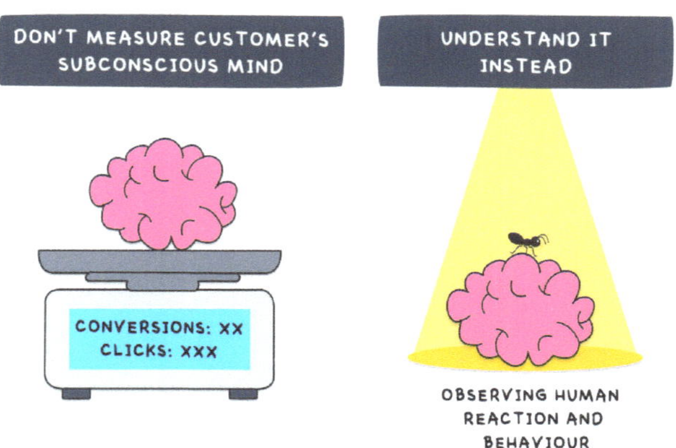

(Continued)

Then, *Magic* happens: attitudes and behaviours can change, and your brand can gain a very positive attitude from customers.

But Magic is hated by people who want a direct connection to results.
Management wants control.
So Management tries to measure a customer's subconscious mind and get a formula.

Getting a *formula* for the subconscious seems to be impossible, or very difficult for the near future.

But what we can do instead is *understand* the subconscious- by deeply observing human reaction and behaviour.
Right from eye tracking, to retina enlargement, or time spent on certain products. We get *clues* through behavioural patterns.

And once we understand the subconscious better, we can start our trials to shape behaviour!

All our favourite, loved brands have understood, and *worked upon* shaping our subconscious.

Make that leap of faith into understanding your customer's subconscious mind.

Don't waste time measuring it. Yet. Tomorrow may be different, but we are here.

Time in Market improves timing the market

I've seen a stand up comedian struggle in her *early* years.
She got a stray laugh or two at times during her act.
Her material was all about teenage angst around friends, parents, and love interests (she's a Gen Z'er)

She kept changing her material, and she *hit* gold when she started talking about jobs, work and related angst.

She's big now- she's got, in marketing parlance, *product- market fit*.
Where the product (her act) succeeded in getting a response from the market (her audience)

You can only know this in hindsight, unless you are an exception.

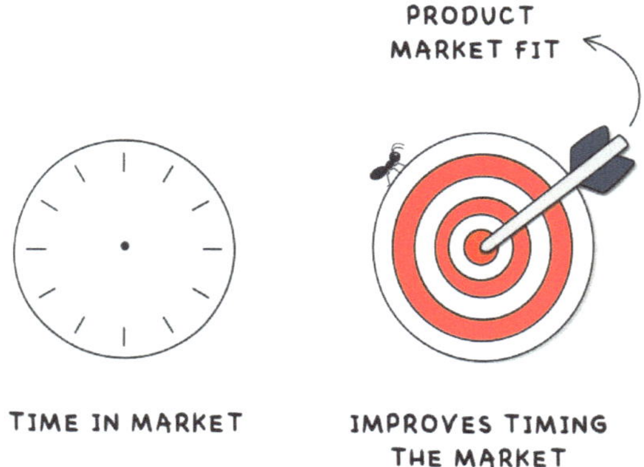

(Continued)

All great companies have worked under the *radar*, trying to figure out what will stick and what doesn't.

YouTube started off as a dating site (!) and pivoted to find its product market fit the way we know it at the moment.

All failed companies remain below the radar, and therefore we don't know about them.

The interesting thing here for a marketer?

Sure, a lot of this is attributable to timing and luck.
But a lot of it is also about knowing that we don't start with gold.
We need to *test* out our stuff, fail, and come back empty handed till we get a semblance of a chance.

The more *time* you spend intelligently learning (at low cost, with testable assumptions, making the right changes and trying again) the better we understand *timing* the market.

Let people then talk about your overnight success.
We only understand product market fit in hindsight.

Every other brand in the market is both your competitor and collaborator

If you're Coke, then Pepsi is your direct competitor.
So is Diet Coke (cannibalisation).
Juices, not so direct. Sparkling water, even less so.

Heck, even a personal trainer advising his trainees to stay away from Soda is a hindrance.

It's a *jungle* out there.

But in this jungle, strange things do happen.

Research has shown that the moment you have a competitor, you *increase* the category of people wanting to buy your kind of product.

Why does this happen?

(Continued)

Let's take an example. The local vegetable market, (Sabzi Mandi in India) or take a Farmer's market somewhere in California. Same difference.

The fact that there are competing sellers of similar (sometimes the same) produce in a market square means that there is more *awareness* about that marketplace.
Competitors actually benefit because they compete, since they raise overall awareness and *ease* of finding vendors.

To add to this, imagine that you have a regular vendor you go to at this Sabzi Mandi, ask for tomatoes, but he's out of stock.
What does he do? He asks for help from his direct competitor, and gives them to you, guaranteeing their freshness and juiciness.

In front of you!
The *competitor* helps your vendor manage his relationship with you.

Why?
Because everyone knows that they might need some help some other day.
It's called *Reciprocal Altruism*, and has helped the human race be what it is.

Doctors help doctors, Lawyers help lawyers, and people change jobs and go to competing companies all the time.
Google needs Apple, Apple needs Meta, Meta needs Amazon, and they all compete with each other.

Every brand in the market is *both* your competitor and collaborator.

Ask not what the customer wants. Ask what the customer wants to be

If you're a comedian, and you ask what jokes your audience would like you to crack, and ask them to kind of give you hints on what the punchline should be, you should choose another profession.

And if you're a marketer, asking your customers questions about which product feature about your brand *they prefer* the most, and what likely price *they would buy* something, and questions like that, you should…

Become a better marketer.

Asking a customer what she wants will get dull, uninspired, *cliched* answers that unfortunately a lot of research throws up.

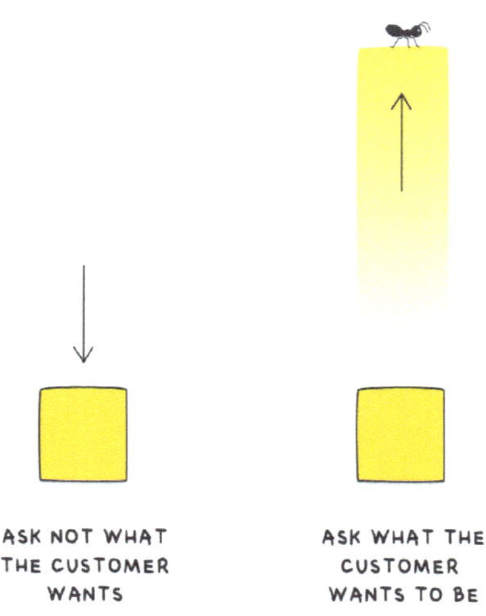

(Continued)

Don't blame her- she's using her *current* reality and *past* experiences to
come up with those.
I mean, you could ask all that, but don't stop there.
Or don't even start, because the information you will probably get will *confirm*
what you know already.

What use is that?

Asking a customer what she *wants to be*, however,
Will unlock a lot of aspects about a customer that will not only surprise you,
But also surprise the customer herself.

 It's because she's using her imagination and she's opening up about her
dreams and aspirations.
You could end up with net *new insights*.

This will inspire you to come up with the right offering and the right way to
converse with her.
It will *elevate* your brand to a new association.

That association will be the most useful to be a meaningful part of her life
that's about to unfold.
Your brand will then belong with her *future* self.

Build it and they will definitely not come

Seen the movie "Field of Dreams"?
This Kevin Costner, baseball- inspired movie was all about a singular man having a grand vision about building a baseball stadium in the middle of nowhere.

This inspiration was captured in the famous movie quote:
"Build it, and they will come".

This was movie magic at its best, and inspired a lot of businesses to go ahead with amazing visions about their products and create them.
It inspired a lot of tech entrepreneurs, including silicon valley, till *reality* set in:

If you build your product first, there are high chances that you won't get any customers, unless you are very lucky or a visionary with great timing.

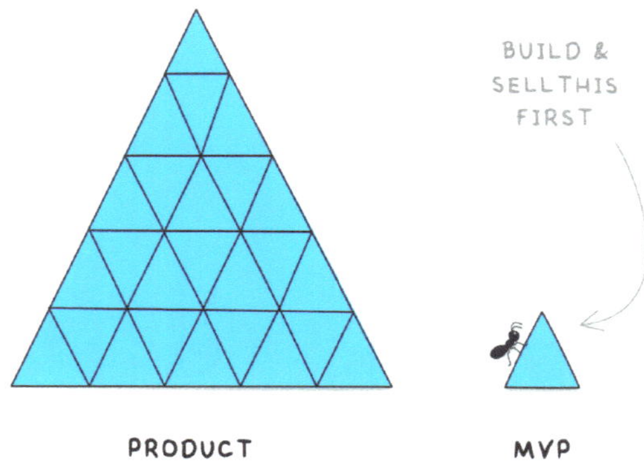

(Continued)

If you build it first, however strong your vision may be, you could be *hallucinating*. And no, market research may *not* be the only or best way to mitigate this risk.

Why do we insist on knowing that we are on the right path?
This **provider-centric** thinking appears because:
We *imagine* a world where our perfect product will meet the perfect customer in the perfect setting as seen by us.

Then Mike Tyson punches us in the face, and we realise that we need another path.
The next time you feel that you have a product vision that is amazing, and the "Field of Dreams" comes to mind to inspire you, remember:

It's a movie.

You could try what Airbnb did.

Put up a simple website about your own lodgings to rent them out, for a conference in your city, to see if people *see the value* that you see in your idea.

That's a **minimum viable product**, and its way better than the movie.

Customers will believe you to be more honest if you tell them you've been lying to them

Imagine a commercial starring your local politician:

"I believe in radical honesty… Mahatma Gandhi believed in speaking the *truth*, and so do I…. The *truth* and nothing but the *truth*, that's what I stand for… Honesty is better than cleanliness and godliness.."

What's the *first* thought that comes to your mind?

What a goddamn liar this person is.

Customers suss you out. They will *not believe* you if you tell them you are honest.

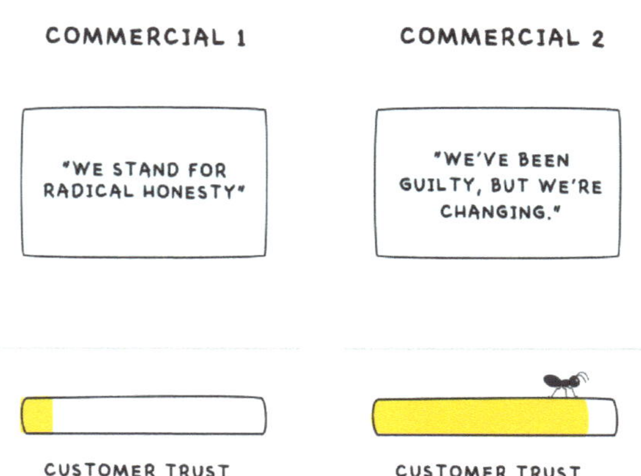

(Continued)

On the other hand, if you tell them this, through an ad on your fashion brand's take on the environment:

"We aren't doing enough, and we think we've been like ostriches, robbing the earth's precious resources for future generations through our products.
We think our entire industry can change its ways, but we don't want to wait.
We want to raise our hand and fess up.
We have been guilty, but no more of that. I'm sure you don't believe our words. Heck, we won't believe us if we were in your shoes. So we'd let our actions speak. Here's what we plan to *actively* do…"

Chances are, they will believe you to be *more* honest than usual, and possibly support you.

Is this reverse psychology, where we are treating customers like children, getting them to eat their veggies by saying they are horrible, don't eat them?

No.

In fact, this is about treating customers as intelligent people, who need to be spoken to with candour and authenticity.

Customers will give you a *chance* if you level with them and do something real and vulnerable, and daring.

Get new customers to keep your existing ones with you

Common sense tells us that we shouldn't get new customers at the expense of pissing off existing ones.

For example, the existing customers of a bank will get sore about the bank offering more attractive terms to new customers.

Existing customers of a telecom service will get angry if you discount new customers more.

And even if you don't offer them discounts or freebies, just focusing on new customers will make your existing customers feel neglected. *Right?*

This will lead to them leaving you and going to competition. *Right?*

Wrong. In both cases.

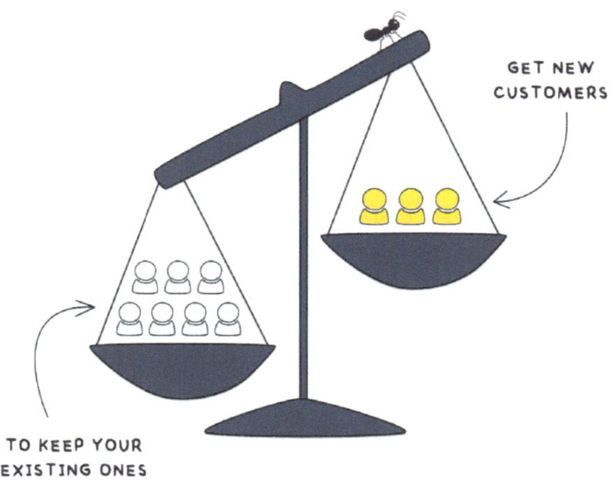

(Continued)

All the marketing rules get turned over on their head when we see *data*.

What we now know is that the best way to get existing customers to be loyal with you is if you rapidly get new customers.
(You can read more about Byron Sharp's seminal work on How Brands work for proof, or just trust me on this one!)

Why does this happen? I'm not sure what Byron Sharp says, butI suspect this is because of:

Switching costs: Costs associated with the time, effort and money spent on going with competition

Risks and inertia: Who knows how the unknown devil will be like? Also, I really don't want to think about this choice beyond a point. It's too painful.

And most of all,

Confirmation bias: If I'm an existing customer, I believe in my brand more if I see more people choose it.

When you see a large crowd behind you, you find more courage to stick with your decision.

Getting a crowd of new customers is the best way of keeping your existing ones with you.

Any last words, Travelling Professor?

Thank you, Moina Abdul, former student, co-conspirator, designer of *awesome* illustrations and gentle feedback giver to this book.

Thank you, dear reader, for buying and hopefully buying *into* the ideas presented in this book.

(Also, do check my other book: **Not a Self Help Book**, the first book, which are observations on LIFE, if you like this one)

More Notes on Marketing to come soon? We're planning a sequel, stay warned!

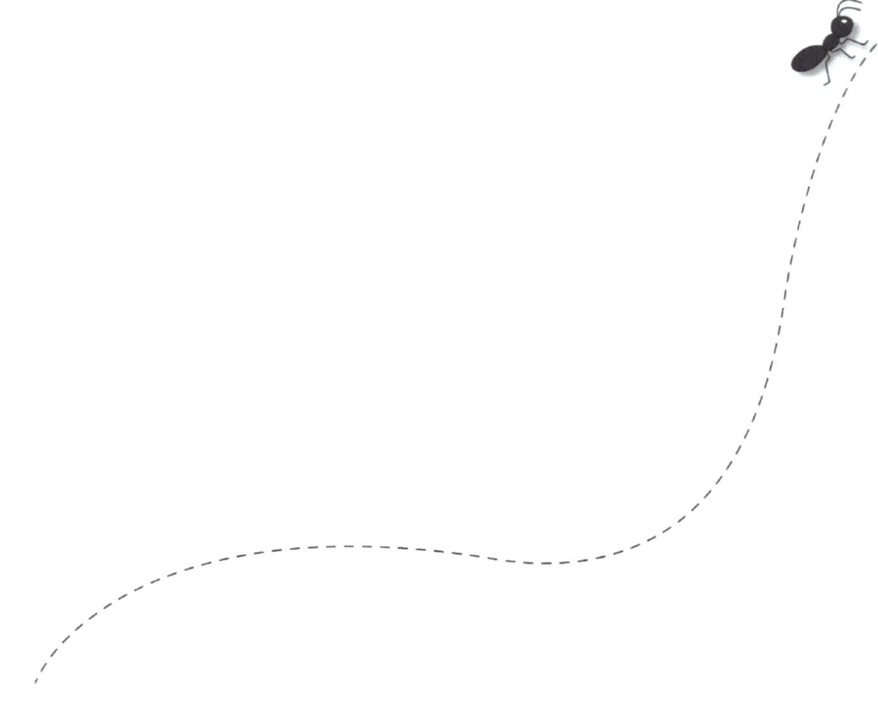